Bulldozers

Aaron Frisch

CREATIVE EDUCATION

seedlings

Published by Creative Education
P.O. Box 227, Mankato, Minnesota 56002
Creative Education is an imprint of
The Creative Company
www.thecreativecompany.us

Design by Ellen Huber
Production by Chelsey Luther
Art direction by Rita Marshall
Printed in the United States of America

Photographs by Alamy (Photoshot Holdings Ltd), Dreamstime
(Anyaivanova, Artzzz), Getty Images (Lorentz Gullachsen,
J. Ronald Lee), iStockphoto (Ahmed Aboul-Seoud, filonmar,
Brandon Laufenberg), Shutterstock (artiomp, Robert J. Beyers
II, Janaka Dharmasena, Jvrublevskaya, Dmitry Kalinovsky,
Art Konovalov, LuckyPhoto, Mike Ludkowski, Robert Pernell,
rtem, Vladimir Sazonov, smereka), SuperStock (age fotostock,
Transtock)

Library of Congress Cataloging-in-Publication Data
Frisch, Aaron.
Bulldozers / Aaron Frisch.
p. cm. — (Seedlings)
Summary: A kindergarten-level introduction to bulldozers,
covering their size, movement, role in the process of
construction, and such defining features as their crawler
tracks and blades.
Includes bibliographical references and index.
ISBN 978-1-60818-338-8
1. Bulldozers—Juvenile literature. I. Title.

TA725.F75 2013
629.225—dc23   2012023247

First Edition
9 8 7 6 5 4 3 2 1

TABLE OF CONTENTS

Time
to push!

Bulldozers are strong machines. They push dirt.

They knock down trees.

A bulldozer has a big blade on the front. It has special wheels.

The wheels are called crawler tracks.

Crawler tracks are strong.

They help bulldozers go over bumpy ground.

Some bulldozers have a ripper. It is on the back. A ripper can break concrete.

Bulldozers can be big or small.

Some bulldozers use a bucket. The bucket can carry rocks.

A bulldozer makes the ground flat. Then other machines can do work there.

All done
pushing!

Picture a Bulldozer

exhaust pipe

ripper

crawler tracks

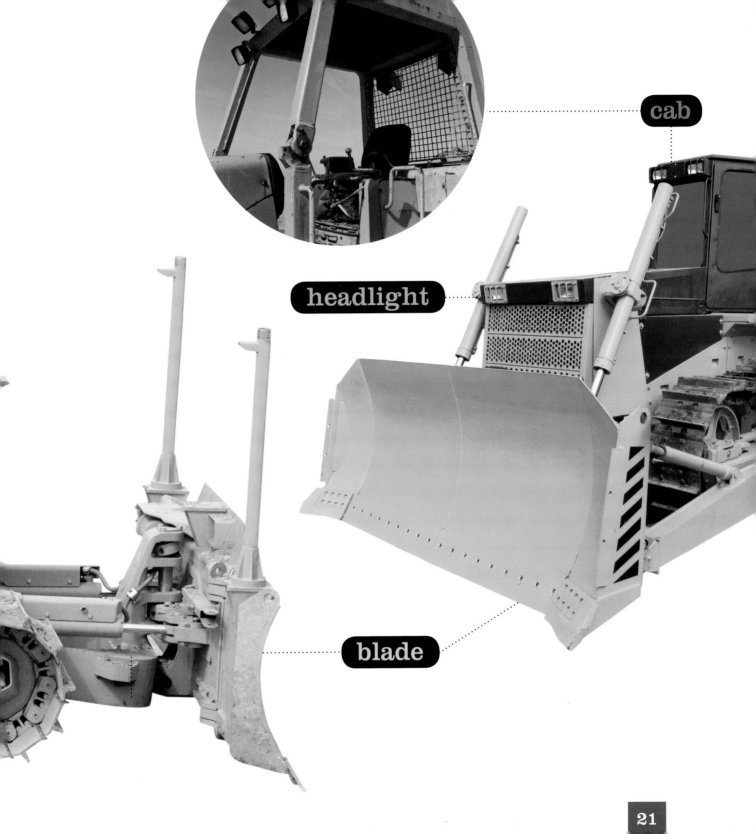

cab

headlight

blade

Words to Know

blade: a hard, flat object

concrete: a super hard material used to make sidewalks and roads

crawler tracks: big, strong belts that go around like wheels

ripper: a tool used to break hard things

Read More

Martin, M. T. *Bulldozers.*
Minneapolis: Bellwether, 2007.

Sobel, June. *B Is for Bulldozer: A Construction ABC.*
San Diego: Gulliver Books, 2003.

Websites

Big Trucks for Kids
http://www.bigtrucksforkids.com/bulldozer-videos.html
This site has pictures and videos of bulldozers at work.

Construction Coloring Pages
http://www.coloring.ws/construction1.htm
This site has bulldozer pictures. You can print and color them.

Index